Life Cycle of a

Pumpkin

Ron Fridell
and
Patricia Walsh

Heinemann
LIBRARY

www.heinemann.co.uk/library
Visit our website to find out more information about Heinemann Library books.

To order:

☎ Phone 44 (0) 1865 888066

🖹 Send a fax to 44 (0) 1865 314091

🖳 Visit the Heinemann Bookshop at www.heinemann.co.uk/library to browse our catalogue and order online.

First published in Great Britain by Heinemann Library, Halley Court, Jordan Hill, Oxford OX2 8EJ
a division of Reed Educational and Professional Publishing Ltd.
Heinemann is a registered trademark of Reed Educational & Professional Publishing Ltd.

OXFORD   MELBOURNE   AUCKLAND   JOHANNESBURG   BLANTYRE   GABORONE
IBADAN   PORTSMOUTH (NH) USA   CHICAGO

Designed by Wilkinson Design
Illustrated by David Westerfield
Originated by Dot Gradations
Printed by South China Printing in Hong Kong.

ISBN 0431 08460 2 (hardback)   ISBN 0431 08461 0 (paperback)
05 04 03 02   06 05 04 03 02
10 9 8 7 6 5 4 3   10 9 8 7 6 5 4 3 2 1

British Library Cataloguing in Publication Data

Fridell, Ron
   Life cycle of a pumpkin
   1. Pumpkin
   I. Title   II. Walsh, Patricia
   583.6'3

Acknowledgements
The Publisher would like to thank the following for permission to reproduce photographs:
Corbis /Mark Gibson p.29, /Philip Gould p.21, /Richard Hamilton Smith p.27, /Matthew Klein p.23, /Barry Lewis p.22, /Richard T. Nowitz p.26, /Reuters New Media Inc. p.18, /Phil Schermeister p.5; Index Stock/Steve Solum pp.12, 28, /Shmuel Taylor p. 10; Dwight Kuhn pp.7, 8, 9, 11, 14, 15, 19, 20, 25, 28, 29; Ben Klaffe pp.4, 13, 16, 17, 29; Photodisc/Santokh Kochar pp.6, 28; PhotoEdit/PictureQuest/Tony Freeman p.24.

Cover photograph reproduced with the permission of Dwight Kuhn.

Every effort has been made to contact copyright holders of any material reproduced in this book. Any omissions will be rectified in subsequent printings if notice is given to the Publisher.

Some words are shown in bold, **like this**. You can find out what they mean by looking in the Glossary.

Contents

What is a pumpkin?

A pumpkin is a fruit that people use for food. It grows on a **vine**. People plant pumpkins in fields. Each year there is a new **crop**.

Seed

1 week

2 weeks

10 weeks

There are many different kinds of pumpkin.
They can be bumpy or smooth, large or
small, long or round. They can be orange,
white, yellow, or red.

11 weeks

14 weeks

16 weeks

Seed

Pumpkins begin as **seeds.** The seeds are white and have an **oval** shape. A tiny plant is curled up inside each seed.

Seed

1 week

2 weeks

10 weeks

The seed is planted in warm, moist soil.
In about ten days, a root grows down
into the soil to take in water and food
for the plant. The seed splits, and tiny
leaves push up into the sunlight.

11 weeks

14 weeks

16 weeks

Seedling

The first two leaves push through the soil. These are smooth **seed** leaves. They use sunlight and air to make food for the new pumpkin plant.

8

Seed

I week

2 weeks

10 weeks

Then the other leaves appear. They are jagged and prickly. The job of the seed leaves is done. They **wither** and fall off.

11 weeks

14 weeks

16 weeks

Vine early summer

The pumpkin plant grows more leaves. The plant grows quickly and soon becomes a **vine.** The vine twists and creeps along the ground.

Seed

I week

2 weeks

10 weeks

The vine sends out thin **tendrils.** They will grab and curl around other vines, or twist around fences. They support the vine as it grows longer and longer.

11 weeks

14 weeks

16 weeks

Flower   early summer

The pumpkin **vine** has many yellow flowers. Some of these are **female** flowers. Female flowers sit on small, fuzzy green balls.

Seed

1 week

2 weeks

10 weeks

The **male** flowers are on long stems and have yellow powder inside the flower. The yellow powder is **pollen.** It takes a male and a female flower to make a pumpkin.

11 weeks

14 weeks

16 weeks

Pollination

Bees also help to make pumpkins. They move the **pollen** from **male** flowers to **female** flowers. When a bee visits the male flowers, the pollen sticks to the bee's body and legs.

Seed

1 week

2 weeks

10 weeks

The pollen rubs off the bee's legs as it goes in and out of the flowers. When the pollen reaches a female flower, the fuzzy green ball at the end of the flower begins to grow into a pumpkin.

11 weeks   14 weeks   16 weeks

Growing and ripening

16

All summer the **vines**, **tendrils** and leaves of the plant grow and tangle together. Underneath the big leaves are little green pumpkins.

Seed

1 week   2 weeks

10 weeks

The leaves are like big umbrellas. They keep the hot sun off the pumpkins. They also help to keep the soil around the pumpkins from drying out.

11 weeks

14 weeks

16 weeks

Problems for pumpkins

Growing pumpkins need just the
right amount of water and sun.
Too much rain **rots** the pumpkins.
Too much sun **withers** the **vines**.

Seed

I week

2 weeks

10 weeks

Cucumber beetles and **squash** bugs can damage pumpkins, too. Farmers spray the plants with **insecticides**, or cover the vines with nets to protect the growing pumpkins.

11 weeks   14 weeks   16 weeks

Harvest

20

The pumpkins grow bigger and bigger. Their skin changes from green to orange. Inside each pumpkin, the **seeds** and **pulp** begin to grow.

Seed

I week

2 weeks

10 weeks

Then the **vines** begin to turn brown.
Harvest time has come. The farmer cuts
the thick pumpkin stem from the vine.

11 weeks

14 weeks

16 weeks

After the harvest

Now the farmer has **harvested** the pumpkins. They will be sold at supermarkets and farm shops. Some pumpkins will be sent to other countries to be sold.

Seed

1 week

2 weeks

10 weeks

People use pumpkins to make pumpkin pie, soup and bread. In countries that grow many pumpkins, they are also fed to farm animals.

11 weeks

14 weeks

16 weeks

What happens next

In some countries people have contests to find out who grew the biggest pumpkin.

Seed

I week

2 weeks

10 weeks

For Hallowe'en, on 31 October, many people scoop out pumpkins and carve them to make lanterns. People put candles inside to make the lanterns glow with a warm, orange light.

11 weeks

14 weeks

16 weeks

Inside the pumpkin are many **seeds.** Some are roasted and eaten as a snack. Others are saved and planted in the spring. These seeds will grow into next year's pumpkins.

Seed

1 week

2 weeks

10 weeks

After the pumpkins are picked and sold, the farmer **ploughs** the field. Any old **vines** and left-over fruit are mixed with the soil. The field is ready for planting seeds again next spring.

11 weeks

14 weeks

16 weeks

Life cycle

1 Seed

2 Seedling

3 Vine and flower

4 Pollination

5 Growing pumpkin

6 Harvest

Fact file

- The biggest pumpkin on record was grown in Ontario, Canada, in 1998. It weighed as much as a large horse!

- The kind of pumpkin in this book usually weighs as much as two or more large bags of sugar.

- A pumpkin **vine** might have flowers all summer, but each flower lasts for only one day.

- North America, Europe and Great Britain grow the most pumpkins.

Glossary

crop food grown in one season

female girl or woman

harvest gathering of a crop

insecticide poison that kills insects

male boy or man

oval round shape, longer than it is wide

plough turn and mix soil before planting

pollen grains of yellow powder that are released from male flowers

pulp soft, fleshy part of a fruit or vegetable

rot spoil

seed part of a plant that can grow into a new plant

squash fruit like a pumpkin that tastes sweeter, and is popular in America

tendril long, thin part of a plant stem that grabs and curls around things to help the plant climb

vine plant with long, thin stems that grow along the ground or climb up things

wither dry up, shrivel

Index